DASJATI • HALFWAY TO HEAVEN

published by
Diplodocus Press
Bangkok • Los Angeles

ISBN: trade paperback
9781940999470
ISBN: hardcover
9781940999432

© 2019 by Bangkok Opera Foundation

First Edition • Revised

0 9 8 7 6 5 4 3 2

DAS·JATI

Halfway to Heaven

*A Photographic Report on
The Ten Lives of the Buddha Project
at the half-way mark*

compiled by S.P. Somtow

'THAYREUTH' CYCLE

Sucharitkul is already well on the way to fulfilling an even more ambitious project: nothing less than the most extended music drama of all time, exceeding even the *Ring*, consisting of 10 linked works of opera, ballet, opera-ballet and other forms as yet unhybridised. The *DasJati* cycle tells the 'Ten Lives of the Buddha', familiar stories in Buddhist culture. By the year 2020, it will form the basis of a five-day performance-cycle and festival, a sort of Bangkok Bayreuth, focusing the eyes of the world's artistic community on Thailand in a bold new way. First to be performed was *The Silent Prince*, in Houston in 2012, then came *Mahajanaka* in 2014 and *Bhuridatta* and *Suwana Sama* in 2015. The latest, *Nemiraj*, will be premiered in Bangkok this year.

Apart from Sucharitkul's own operas and Wagner, productions have included Mozart and Puccini standards, along with *Carmen, Otello, Dido and Aeneas, La Calisto, Turn of the Screw, Rape of Lucretia* and somewhat rarer works such as *Bluebeard's Castle, Prima La Musica, The Impresario, Thaïs, Savitri*, Hans Krasà's *Brundibár* and Grigory Frid's *The Diary of Anne Frank*.

It's a daring adventure, a breathtaking leap of ambition, an amazing "gift to the world" from a small country that may seem to some to be far from the world's operatic center.

It's a new way to bring to news audiences the most iconic stories of Theravada Buddhism, told and retold for thousands of years, in the language of music, singing, drama, and dance, a language that belongs to every culture in the world — yet the particular dialect of this language is equal parts Asia and Europe.

Halfway through this journey, let's take a moment to look at all that has already been achieved.

Five linked works of music drama — from the oratorio-like *Mahajanaka* to the intimate chamber opera *The Silent Prince,* from the childlike simplicity of *The Faithful Son* to the convoluted machinations of *The Dragon Lord,* to the cosmic allegory of *Chariot of Heaven.*

There has been a hiatus for almost two years, but now it's time for final five music dramas to emerge, and 2019 will see premieres of two of them: the short ballet *Chandakumar* and the magically complex *Architect of Dreams.*

Wagner finished the second work in *The Ring* in 1856 and didn't complete the third until 1871 — a fifteen year gap. *The Ring* took twenty-six years to finish. *DasJati* is going relatively quickly, but in fact the first music, for *Mahajanaka,* was composed in 1996 and incorporated into the *DasJati* project in 2014. So in a sense this work will have taken as long as *The Ring* to complete.

The difference is, in 1996 I didn't know I was going in the direction of such a massive, integrated work.

The main thing is this: I have entered the third and presumably "final" act of my life. I had a first act in Europe with a little intermezzo in Thailand in the 1970s, a second act in America mostly working as a novelist, and now I've come home. This work is what I would like to give back to the place I came from. My chosen genres may seem European or American, but the roots of my art are Thai.

— *Somtow Sucharitkul*

> Somtow could not have come up with a better endorsement of the triumphant power of the path to love and truth. "The Silent Prince" is an extraordinary achievement for Thailand, and a gift to the world.
>
> — THE NATION

The Silent Prince
เตมียใบ้

Riding the Lightning
hubris and humility

*text of a TEDx Talk given in Chiengmai, January 2016
by Somtow Sucharitkul*

It's said that lightning doesn't strike the same place twice. As artists, we are told that inspiration is like lightning: we wait on a hilltop until one day the spark comes that brings with it achievements, riches, and fame.

The truth, as any pilot will tell you, is that lightning strikes the same place all the time. So do those bolts of inspiration. It's what we do with that spark that I want to talk about.

Everyone here today has had at one time or another been struck with "a big idea" — one that by its very nature must change the way the world perceives reality. A "big idea" starts with "what if?" — "What if people could fly?" — "What if the earth went around the sun?" — "What if we had a play in which the words were all sung?"

For every "big idea" that springs to life, there are countless others that are not acted on. All of you have had these ideas, not once, but often. These ideas are frightening because by their very nature they must change the world in some manner, large or small — whether it's a moon landing or an auto-flush toilet.

We fear to bring these ideas about. But once in a while, we are driven to do so. This is how one such idea came into being, teased at the periphery of my brain for some years, and then in a single moment was made flesh.

For the past five years, I have been working on "the biggest work of music drama in history" — but I didn't know for four and a half of those years.

Most musicians and fans of classical music know that "the biggest work of music drama in history" is Wagner's monumental *Ring* cycle. This work is so big that it takes four evenings to perform. It uses an orchestra of about 120 people. It tells a story that begins with the dawn of the gods and ends with the destruction of the universe. It is an icon of European, and specifically German culture. An entire town in Southern Germany, Bayreuth, is devoted to producing it and other Wagner operas, and there is a ten year waiting list for tickets.

Composing the *Ring* took decades of Wagner's life and it is one of the summits of European artistic achievement. Wagner's dream, to integrate poetry, music, and theater in a new fusion, instigated an artistic revolution that is felt not just in opera, but even in art forms that did not exist in Wagner's lifetime, such as film.

Disputing Wagner, let alone toppling him, was furthest from my mind when, in 2009, I received an request from a progressive opera company inTexas, to compose a small-scale opera. The only condition was that it would have something to do with India.

The Silent Prince, the work I created for this company, is adapted from *DasJati,* the collection of ten notable lives of the Buddha which is a centerpiece of Theravada Buddhism. They are ten central myths of our culture and of the entire world Buddhist community. *The Silent Prince,* adapted from the first of the ten stories, tells of a prince whose proud father tells him to order a criminal'd execution. To disobey one's father is a terrible karmic sin. To kill a man, equally sinful. Prince Temiya's deals with the moral conflict by retreating into silence.

At first the story seems far removed from our world. But today, when a child faces a intolerable dilemma and flees into an inner world, we give it a fancy name; autism perhaps. So, I wrote an opera about mythology that was also about dysfunctional families and traumatized children. It was a Buddhist parable about the contemporary world. It was, indeed, the first specifically Buddhist opera to hit the western world.

The premiere was rewarded with great reviews: the best I'd ever received. *The Silent Prince* was widely viewed as a breakthrough in my operatic career, but it was far from a project to change the world.

A few years later, we had a political upheaval in his country, and a huge international choir festival I had planned for Bangkok was about to be canceled because of travel anxiety. The Ministry of Culture said to me, "Isn't there something you could do that would use local singers, yet open a window for them to still come to Thailand?"

Thus it was that I resurrected my *Mahajanaka Symphony,* composed for the King's 60 birthday, composed in 1997 as a meditation on His Majesty's *own* meditation on the second of the ten DasJati tales — the story of a prince who braves the impossible, literally "takes up arms against a sea of troubles," and breaks through to a divine intervention. To recast this work as a drama instead of pure symphonic music, I introduced the element of narrative dance. The full length narrative ballet is a moribund art form in the west. But the Buddhist imagery gave the genre a new perspective.

I had at that point adapted two of the ten great lives of the Buddha into some kind of music-theatrical incarnation, and now I was deeply into the

from the Bayreuth premiere, 2016

from the Bayreuth premiere, 2016

jataka tales, marvelling at their relevance to modern life, understanding they are an inheritance that constantly renews itself. I picked another jataka tale to adapt — the story of *Bhuridat*, a prince of nagas, who is captured by an unscrupulous snake charmer and forced to dance to the sound of a magic pipe for the amusement of peasants in village squares and to the enrichment of his captor.

It was then that the bolt of lightning came. I was assailed by an attack of megalomania — even hubris, because the inspiration also involved a challenge to the unchallenged gods of music.

Why stop at three operas? Why not set all ten of the Ten Lives of the Buddha to music? Why not add dance to Wagner's fusion of music, poetry and drama, and create an even richer fusion — a new art form?

A work that combined those four art forms, and consisted of ten full length productions which could be performed as a connected whole, perhaps over a seven day period, would be by definition the largest ever conceived in the history of live performance. And if there were a festival, say, every three years, in which the entire Ten Lives of the Buddha were performed, would that not make Thailand into a mecca for lovers of opera and dance? Would it not provide employment for singers, directors, dancers, musicians, set designers, costume designers, and interpreters — not just on a one time basis, but for generations to come? Would not the entire fabric of the cultural universe be bent towards a part of the world not previously thought to be a world operatic center? Would the existence of this work not imprint Thailand permanently on the world's cultural community?

That, in short, is the "hubris" part of the lightning. Now, the "humility."

— It's too big. Well, yes, obviously it is too big. It's a new art form *and* it's ten full length works.

— It's too difficult. Yes. Each of the ten stories is as complicated as the entire *Ring* cycle. Extracting the contemporary resonance from each piece and connecting them so that the entire seven-day event is clearly woven from a single skein of fabric requires holding a lot of jigsaw pieces in one's head.

— It's too impractical. Putting on one opera is bad enough — let alone an opera plus dance — with maybe 200-300 performers in some cases. Putting on ten means a cast of thousands. How many rehearsals?

— I don't have the resources. Something like this costs money, which doesn't grow on trees.

— I am not worthy. One looks at the giants of the past and wonders how one had the gall to think one could take them on. The weight of all that past achievement is a crushing burden.

So how does one handle the hubris? And how does one cope with the humility? Shall we start with the humility?

Is it too big? Of course it is. Is it too difficult? Of course it is. Is it impractical? Naturally. Am I unworthy to tie the shoelaces of the greats? Arguable, but without the judgment of history, let us assume that, too, is true.

I have learned that *most* of us don't actually want to *be* writers or composers. We want, rather, to *have written.* We want to jump through the hoop that is all the hard work, and fast forward to the acclaim and the money.

So first get this into your head: you are bringing this idea to fruition precisely *because* it is difficult, and complex, and daunting, expensive, and unprecedented — and that it is hard work to go through all those hoops.

When you start telling people about this idea, they will almost certainly not see what is in your head, because, let's face it, it's in *your* head, not theirs. Coupled with the skepticism of the outside world, there's also your own skepticism.

So why *should* we seize these bolts of lightning? Why *do* we go through the angst of seeing them through?

Because in the moment that lightning strikes you, you are the only person in the universe who can act. You are alone. You are the only person who can make it come to life, or consign it to the eternal void. No one can be God for all eternity, but in that singularity of spacetime, you *are* God.

One nanosecond later, you are just a mortal like anyone else.

Hubris — the Greek word for daring to challenge the fates, the gods, our own miserable destinies as specks of dust in a vast uncaring cosmos — is usually considered a bad thing, but now you're going to need it. It is indeed, the only way that you will ever be crazy enough to take the kind of chances that can change the world.

What will you gain? I regret to tell you that to hope for fame or wealth is not something that should be at the top of your list. If you look throughout history, you will see that it's usually the second person to take up a "big idea" that gets these things. The original creator often perishes in obscurity. If you're *really* lucky, you could even get burned at the stake.

If the idea is really big, don't worry about getting rewarded in this lifetime. If it happens, it's gravy.

I want to conclude with the story of a "big idea" that came simultaneously to three composers in the 1970s in Thailand — Bruce Gaston, Dnu Huntrakul, and me. We planned to revolutionize all music in Asia by creating a new fusion between Thai and Western music. Our revolution was to have its Big Bang during a music festival we planned in 1978, attended by almost all the major composers in the region.

The revolution was a bust, you see. The traditional Thai musicians I hired to play with the classical ones walked out. The papers blasted us. The Department of Fine Arts, on opening night, hid the piano and informed me that it had been scientifically determined that modern music would damage its strings.

The three of us were traumatized. We all found different ways to burn out. Bruce and Dnu went in a more commercial direction; I gave up music completely and started a new career as a science fiction writer, running away to America. The revolution was a flop.

As a new century dawned and I visited Thailand after a twenty-five year self imposed exile, I realized to my amazement that, over time, the revolution had in fact succeeded. The fusion of Thai and western musical styles was now so taken for granted that pop music and even TV commercials could freely make use of it. The revolution had permeated so profoundly into the culture that no one was even aware that a revolution had occurred, or that it had once even been necessary for a revolution to occur.

I want to tell you that this is the greatest reward that a "big idea" can ever bring. For you will have changed people's perception of the world so much that they no longer know that their perceptions were changed.

That is the ultimate revolution. The greatest ideas, from relativity to the Eroica Symphony — are facts of life. We cannot really conceive a world without them. They have been woven into the fabric of reality.

If this irony doesn't frighten you — then by all means — *be* God for a nanosecond. Grasp the lightning. Ride it. Hurl it into an unready world. I dare you.

The orchestra prepares for the premiere in Brno, Czech Republic

The Silent Prince • World Premiere • Houston, Texas 2010 • Zilka Hall

The Silent Prince (2009-10)
Houston • The Beginning

The catalyst for *DasJati* was an idea in the mind of Houston based opera conductor Viswa Subbaraman, who commissioned Somtow in 2009 to compose an opera on "any subject, as long as it is set in India."

Somtow had always wanted to deal with the subject of Prince Temiya, the Silent Prince, because as an opera it would provide one amazing challenge: the main character, after all, is "silent" until the last ten minutes of the story. What is an opera if the main character cannot sing? The technical challenge let Somtow to compose the part of the Bodhisattva for a high countertenor or adult male soprano — a voice so unusual and so rare that it would be "worth the wait."

There were other technical challenges; Opera Vista is one of those "maverick" companies with limited means and huge ambitions, and who specialized in world premieres — in other words, the opposite of the average mainstream American opera company. Somtow, who specializes in orchestrating for very large forces, had to rethink his entire sonic palette. *The Silent Prince* is scored for nine solo strings, one each of all the normal wind instruments, keyboards, harp and a few percussionists. From this tiny ensemble, he had to create an impression of lushness, of exotic grandeur — and opera that, as befit its subject

matter, could not seem small in any way

There were delays and obstacles; the entire opera was shelved for over a year and when it was finally mounted it was one night only and in a different theatre than originally planned.

But from this small beginning came something mighty, just as in the parable of the mustard seed.

Without Houston, the entire concept would never have been born. And without the incredible reviews engendered by Houston, and the sold-out hall, there would have been no belief that the world had need of operas about Buddhism.

Production photos from *The Silent Prince*, 2010 production, Zilka Hall, Houston

Sucharitkul disperses a misconception that contemporary opera is esoteric and impertinent. A world premiere perfect for the Houston stage, the rich and exotic sonorities created by juxtaposing delicious instruments like the traditional Indian tambura with celeste, the church-like harmonium and harp with colorful coloratura flourishes, the effect was mesmerizing capturing an honest, respectful and modern representation of Asian culture.

— Culturemap Houston

Stunning, Sensational, and Successful....

Somtow Sucharitkul's *sumptuous and marvelously lyrical score is enchanting (several traditional Indian instruments are used in the orchestra---tamburas, celeste, harmonium), moving, intriguing, and always retains a deep sense of mystery and spirituality. His rich and beautiful orchestrations are masterful, meaningful, and mesmerizing.*

— Houston Chronicle

The two-hour score spikes lush Western sonorities with tangy Asian elements. The tambura's drone, along with melismas and undulating vocal lines, wafts incense over the mystical proceedings.

— Opera Magazine, London

Viswa Subbaraman speaks about *DasJati*

An Interview with *DasJati's* first conductor

You were instrumental in bringing the *DasJati* project into existence. How did it happen?

When I ran Opéra Vista, I was asked to see whether it was possible to put together an opera based on an Indian story. Honestly, I googled to see who might have written one, and I came across Somtow's *Ayodhya*. Oddly, Somtow and I were already friends on Facebook, so I messaged him to see whether he'd be able to reduce Ayodhya to a chamber size. Somtow made the fatal mistake of saying that it would be much easier to write a new opera. He mentioned he had been thinking of writing an opera based on the Jataka Tale about the Silent Prince, and the opera was born.

Did you realize at the time that this would be the first Buddhist opera ever produced?

I don't think either of us realized it would become part of such a monumental opéra cycle. Shortly after the premiere Somtow mentioned the Das Jati project, and it took off.

What was your reaction on receiving the score?

Haha! I think I was just happy receiving parts of the score. We would receive a portion and directly send it to the singers. Honestly, though, I was amazed. Somtow had melded aspects of Indian Carnatic music, western classical, and other Asian styles to create a unique but taught work. It told the story beautifully and had such dramatic pacing. I was also impressed with the use of the small orchestra. He was able to extract so many colors from the forces we had at our disposal.

What were some of the difficulties in bringing the score to the performing stage?

At the time, our biggest difficulty was budget. We were a small upstart little start up company. We didn't have money to throw at problems, so we had to be smart.

At first Houston doesn't seem like the likeliest place for an opera like *The Silent Prince* to premiere. What was Houston's reaction?

I think Houston gets a bum rap at times. Houston has a large Indian community and the second largest Asian community after Los Angeles. That being said, most of our audience was a standard white opera going public. The reaction was thunderous, frankly. The audience loved the work.

How has the *DasJati* project impacted you personally and professionally?

The *DasJati* project has been an important one for Asian opera. We need more operas in the répertoire told from an Asian perspective that don't simply use Asian themes to create "exoticism". As for me personally, I'm proud to be behind the genesis of the project, and I hope to be part of future DasJati cycles - especially if and when the cycle is promoted outside of Asia.

The Silent Prince (2012)

Then Director-General of the Department of Cultural Promotion, Prisna Pongtadsirikul, asked Somtow to produce an event in honour of Thailand's National Day, the birthday of His Majesty King Rama IX. This turned out to be the real genesis of *DasJati*.

On the opening night, which was the birthday of His Majesty King Rama IX, the Thailand Cultural Center was completely packed. This is something that had never happened for the world premiere of an opera before!

Simulcast on a Buddhist television station, the first opera composed from an entirely Buddhist sensibility only had a single performance on December 5, 2012. It was clearly intended as a one-off, a work composed for Opera Vista in Houston which had been revived for a grand occasion.

But its rapturous reception was prophetic. The retelling of the *Ten Lives of the Buddha* in a new artistic medium, for audience all over the world, was an idea whose time had come, though it took Somtow two more operas before he realized it.

Somtow Transcendent
"The Silent Prince" is a stunning opera - and a lesson for our times

In Somtow Sucharitkul's opera "The Silent Prince", which had its Bangkok premiere at the Thailand Cultural Centre on December 5 in honour of His Majesty the King, Jak Cholvijarn – not just Prince Temiya, the character he played – meditated for almost the entire length of the production. Finally, in the last astonishing five minutes, the Prince revealed himself as a bodhisattva, a man about to become a god.

As in Mozart's operas, where brief silence between notes can speak as eloquently as the music, Jak's enduring quiet made for a transfixing, drawn-out prelude. Temiya withstands incessant distractions and hindrances, then turns to meditate with eyes firmly shut, the better to see the road to becoming the Buddha. Jak, a student of Buddhism, has said that meditating onstage just as surely blocks out distractions so that his soul projects only transcendent good. The power of his silence was riveting.

The show's spirituality was itself a form of meditation, taking audience members to a new understanding of their role in the world. That, Jak explained, was the intention.

Imbued by Wagner, Somtow's newest – and greatest – opera, is composed of the most evocative leitmotifs for violins. It's ethereal, with a seemingly impossible, unworldly beauty, repeatedly drawing the audience to a Buddhist message of goodwill and hope. It's Mozartean in the sense that it operates on many levels, complex sets of themes depicting the battle between good and evil in each of us. "The Silent Prince" is indeed modern-day Mozart: unfathomably profound and yet highly communicative.

Somtow wanted more people to hear about the lives of the Buddha. Temiya was the first of his final 10 reincarnations, a son forced by compassion to disobey his father's command, a sin, to execute a prisoner, also a sin. Temiya retreats into meditation to banish the evil that torments him.

The score was composed with a classicist's clarity, leaving to Trisdee na Patalung and the Siam Philharmonic Orchestra the formidable task of bringing it to life with precision – and without any cloying romance. Trisdee, tolerating my questions while he lay exhausted on a sofa after the performance, acknowledged that the complexity of the music taxed the youthful ensemble pulled into the ranks of world-class musicians.

As Somtow said, the opera has a relatively small cast of 25 performers, but the sound has to be very big. The orchestra's nine strings tackled nine parts in a terrifyingly complex score and the result was quite natural – when not supernatural – leading us into deep reflection. Meanwhile the woodwinds offered intense colour and great beauty and the brass and percussion conjured the forces of Hell with brutish force. It was extraordinary music, played by brilliant musicians!

It is rare when no fault can be found in a production, yet the virtuosity and brilliance in every component of Somtow's tribute to His Majesty allowed for no error.

The cast was as superb as the musicians. Kyu Won Han depicted the King of Banares frustrated and angry that his son, unwilling to kill, would never reign. His singing was savage, wild, gripped in the perverse evil it conveyed, and his acting was top-scale. When the Prince refused to execute the prisoner, the King wielded the knife himself with the insane brutality demanded by Somtow's music.

Grace Echauri, as Temiya's mother Chandra Devi, was of penetrating voice, yet poetically lyrical in her musically and spiritually complex arias. Accompanying her meditating son, Echauri showed immense passion, grace and courage while a gentle harp illuminated Chandra's soul.

Nadlada Thamtanakorm as the Queen of Heaven and Goddess of Illusion was simply stunning. Somtow's high notes for her were reminiscent of Mozart's Queen of the Night – and demanding beyond belief. Nadlada had no trouble at all, in a breathtaking display that puts her in the highest class of today's operatic singers. John Ames, in mellifluous bass voice and direct in his enunciation, brought a depth and celestial presence to the King of Heaven, even if his Queen clearly wore the family trousers!

As Sunanda, whom the King of Benares sends to dig a grave for his son (Somtow's libretto here conveyed the macabre genius of his namesake, horror writer SP Somtow), Duo Pan portrayed the compelling power of evil. He was forced to keep digging amid unbearable guilt. "O darkness, hide my crime," he sang with horrible pain. Drums, dark brass and ethereal strings brought into focus a fantastical world of lost souls until Sunanda was finally released from his obscene task by the power of the Buddha's revelation that it is impossible to dig deep enough to evade the light of truth.

Zion Daoratanahong, as Amba and an apsara, had strong presence both vocally and dramatically. And the choral sound was focused, mysterious and often terrifying.

Yet Jak Cholvijarn's performance as Prince Temiya remained the focus of the whole evening. It was extraordinary to watch him sit in meditation, oblivious of swarming seductresses seeking to arouse him and thus prove he was a normal human being. The girls wrapping around the motionless Temiya was hideously sexual, but Jak's frozen features showed that Temiya was no normal human. His rejection of evil was so sublime and powerful that, when Jak finally sang, it was a revelation.

Jak is a true male soprano, his sound pure, without question the voice of an angel from Heaven. As Jak revealed Temiya to be the Buddha, his singing projected one of the finest moments in the history of opera, spirituality made possible through the greatest of music enriching the best that can be found in humanity. It offered hope that we might all embrace the truth of universal love.

As a tribute to His Majesty, on the very day the King exhorted his devoted people to follow the dharma and hold harmony in their hearts, Somtow could not have come up with a better endorsement of the triumphant power of the path to love and truth. "The Silent Prince" is an extraordinary achievement for Thailand, and a gift to the world.

Mahajanaka
(1997-2014)

The *DasJati* project grew from two seeds: one, *The Silent Prince*, which was originally a one-off piece commissioned in Houston, and *Mahajanaka*, a ballet-opera which was born from a complex political crisis in Thailand.

Starting in the year 2011, Opera Siam had been hosting the International Choir Festival in Bangkok. Created years earlier by Czech impresario company Festa Musicale and the well known Moravian choir conductor Jiří Klimeš, the choir competition in Pattaya had become a fixture of musical life in Thailand, and the festival was a way to expand this outreach to Bangkok. The idea was to have choirs who were coming to the competition anyway join forces to put on a major work which might not otherwise be produceable in Thailand.

The first project was Somtow's *Requiem for the Mother of Songs,* composed in memory of HRH Princess Galyani Vadhana. The second, Mahler's *Symphony of a Thousand.*

In the third year, a military coup occurred which caused some international nervousess and there was a fear among the international choirs of coming to Thailand. The original work planned for the festival was Britten's *War Requiem.* The Ministry of Culture suggested to Somtow that a large scale performance that would not necessarily involve international choirs be created, perhaps as a tourist attraction.

Somtow offered to stage the *Mahajanaka Symphony* as an opera-ballet. Although this work had been composed in 1997 in honour of His Majesty's book *Phra Mahajanaka* which adapted the well known jataka tale for modern audiences, and was not originally a stage work, the adaptation came quite easily. There was a lot of drama implicit the music, but more music was added in order to illustrate the story more clearly — for example, a dramatic storm at sea sequence was added, brilliant choreographed by Puwarate, the Opera's resident choreographer.

From the 2014 performances of
Mahajanaka, Thailand Cultural Center
International Choir Festival

Damian Whiteley speaks about *DasJati*

How did you come to be involved in the DasJati project?

My first contact with Somtow was singing the world premiere of his extremely emotional Japanese opera *Dan no Ura* in 2014. After the success of that I was asked to play the comical evil brahman Alambayana in *Bhuridat* (the 3rd of the cycle which Somtow wrote).

Talk about the various roles you played and which ones you're particularly into.

Alambayana is a lot of fun, a very physical role with an extremely interesting vocal line which delineates the character very clearly. The double role of King of Heaven/King of Kashi in *Suwana Sama* is a very challenging sing with lush lines in the first role and almost G&S patter and coloratura in the second, a comic character who undergoes a stunning redemption at the end of the opera with a beautiful remorse arioso. The various bass roles in *The Silent Prince* (the first of the *DasJati* cycle) are extremely challenging ranging from high lying Indra in the opening scene to the deeper set Death, which with its angular lines against strong orchestral colours is perhaps my favourite to sing. The most recent role in *The Chariot of Heaven* the first time I only played a 'goody' but the compensation was getting a stunning duet to sing with coloratura soprano.

What are your impression of the work itself, so far?

Having now sung in 4 of the 5 written so far, I ask myself what riches are still to come from the music mind of this composer, having heard so many highlights in the pieces so far (the death march in *Suwana Sama*, the 33 Gods scene, the exotic beauty of *The Silent Prince*, the ecstatic Finale of *Bhuridat* to name a few). I am also starting to fathom the dramaturgical arc and profound philosophical themes dealt within the narrative and to admire the web of leitmotivs and musical ideas which could rival that of Wagner's *Ring*.

What were the challenges of working with such an unorthodox company and in such unusual venues?

Needless to say Opera Siam operates on a slim budget and indeed shows that grand opera can be put on within tight timetables and budgets, if the will and creative innovative energy is there. Whilst the two venues in which I have performed (TCC & Rangsit University) are magnificent performing spaces, the rehearsal venues are much smaller and more often improvised which brings a set of unique challenges. "Time becomes Space" could well be the motto of Opera Siam as miracles happen within conditions and timetables that other companies I have worked with would find impossible and too pressured.

You also trained the chorus. What was that like?

I began to work with the chorus during the preparation of *Bhuridat*, and continued in smaller or greater capacity for *Suwana Sama, The Silent Prince* European tour and most recently more intensely for *The Chariot of Heaven*. Apart from of course getting the music learnt and rehearsed, I have tried to put an emphasis on developing the skills of the very young singers who make up the chorus and to encourage them to use their voices in a healthy way whilst still meeting the challenges which Somtow sets them. Their performance in *The Chariot of Heaven* is testament to the wonderful progress the chorus has made and establishes their importance in the company and its raison d'être.

Thailand is rapidly moving into the operatic universe. What does Thailand have to offer, and what lessons does Thailand need to learn?

Thailand has a stunning wealth of natural vocal talent (as well as quite stunning young orchestral musicians!) with the potential to establish a very strong operatic tradition. Emphasis must be put on the methodical development of vocal talents, with both vocal technical tuition at the highest level and performance opportunities catering to every level of development. Language skills (in the sense of operatic diction and comprehension) are most important and need to be addressed. Where practicable, the production process can take more into account the time needed to keep production values high and the singers/musicians/dancers not fatigued from overly intense rehearsal periods, this without losing the particular spontaneity and improvisational strengths which make Thailand unique in the opera world.

Carnegie Hall (2014)
Bhuridat Sneak Preview

As part of its performance at the International Music Festival in New York City in Carnegie Hall, the Siam Sinfonietta performed a sneak preview of the *Baby Dragon Dance* from *Bhuridat*, receiving a standing ovation from a highly enthusiastic audience.

This was the world premiere of the piece which included a fiendishly difficult solo for the unusual piccolo trumpet.

To the right, producer Thaithow Sucharitkul can be seen with Ambassador Norachit and with Deputy Governor of Bangkok, Khun Amorn Kitchawengkul.

Bhuridat (2014)

The third work in the series to appear was *Bhuridat, The Dragon Lord,* which is based on the sixth of the *Ten Lives of the Buddha,* was conceived because Somtow began to study the jatakas in earnest after having created two rather disparate works derived from them.

At that point, there was still no overriding idea that all ten would be created. But something happened about a quarter of the way through the composition. Musical ideas

began linking up between *Mahajanaka, The Silent Prince,* and this opera. The operas were weaving themselves together.

It was at this point the composer suddenly realized that he was on the road to composing all ten of the *Ten Lives of the Buddha.*

As subsequently described in his TedX talk, *Riding the Lightning,* this revelation was both exhilarating and terrifying.

It came to dominate his thinking and thus it was that he began planning to return to the third work in the *DasJati*, the story of young Sama. Since *Bhuridat* is the sixth work in the cycles according to the Buddhist

scriptures, returning to the third would involve a certain amount of musical "retconning".

With the composition of *The Chariot of Heaven* in 2016 and *The Architect of Dreams* in 2019, the cycle is now all in the right order and hastening to its conclusion.

Bhuridat, a story with dragons, magicians, and transformations, was originally chosen by the composer because it was felt to be a story that would appeal to movie-loving modern audiences. The magic duel in the last act has a *Harry Potter* like feel to it and the opera appeals to fantasy lovers.

Sama: The Faithful Son (2015)
World Premiere Rangsit

The simple tale of a boy in a forest who is slain by a trophy-hunting king and brought back to life through the redeeming power of a mother's tears is one of the most popular of the jatakas. It is an extreme contrast to *Bhuridat* with its highly complex narrative — Sama is a childlike tale, quietly moving,

The highlight of *Sama* is the statue coming to life and singing a dramatic aria after sitting still for so long that many audience members believed she was part of the set.

Another telling moment is the mourning dance performed by the animals of the forest to the throbbing notes of a traditional Thai *khlui* or flute.

from *Auditorium Magazine, Berlin*

A Thai Bayreuth in Bangkok? Thai composer Somtow Sucharitkul's wildly ambitious project to stage a cycle of ten operas with SIAM OPERA in 2020 took a step further towards fulfilment with the premiere of the fourth opera in the series – *Suwana Sama, The Faithful Son* in Bangkok (December 5, 6 and 7). The operas present the Ten Lives of the Buddha, familiar stories in Buddhist culture. The first to be performed was *The Silent Prince* in Houston in 2012, then came *Mahajanaka* in 2014 and *Bhuridatta* in 2015 both premiered in Bangkok.

The Wagner comparisons have a relevance, for not only is Sucharitkul half way through a Bangkok Ring Cycle, he is working closely with Bayreuth on a number of projects, including collaborations between the Festival Orchestra and Sucharitkul's own international award-winning youth orchestra, Siam Sinfonietta, who supply so many of the Siam Philharmonic, the orchestra for the operas.

The project is a bold attempt to fuse traditional Asian themes and music with an easily accessible Western, often very lyrical, style. The result, in *Suwana Sama*, as in its predecessors, is a lively, colourful, enjoyable, and ultimately very moving combination of opera and ballet, of the sacred and the profane. All very Thai!

The venue was Rangsit University's brand new SURYADHEP MUSIC SALA OPERA - a highly impressive addition to Bangkok's arts and music venues. It is an 1100 seat auditorium, which nevertheless seems more intimate than many others of a similar size, with a huge stage, both wide and deep, and wonderful acoustics - ideal for Sucharitkul's productions.

Sucharitkul himself directs the opera and Trisdee na Patalung conducts, as he had both *Mahajanaka* and *Bhuridatta*. The opera is scored for two small chamber orchestras, divided on either side of the conductor, with the addition of some traditional Thai instruments, including an extensive percussion section, and the Khlui – a Thai flute – played with haunting poignancy by Somnuek Saeng-Arun.

Potprecha Cholvijarn in the title role, as the incarnation of the Buddha, conveys a suitably unworldly beauty with his light counter tenor voice. Cassandra Black, fresh from singing Tosca with Milwaukee's Skylight Opera, shows mightily impressive self-control as the Messenger of the King of Heaven. She appears as a statue, on-stage throughout the whole opera, unmoving for 70 minutes, until she comes to life at the end singing an extended aria of Wagnerian intensity. Australian bass Damien Whiteley takes on both the sacred and the profane in the dual roles of King of Heaven and the evil King of Karshi. Whiteley's powerful bass and commanding presence provide the backbone of the opera. There was an impressive appearance, too, from Kaleigh Ray Gamaché, also from Skylight Opera, who produced a strikingly pure-toned freshness in the roles of Apsara and the Queen of Karshi.

There were also encouragingly fine performances in more minor roles by the ensemble of promising young Thai singers, and a chorus showing a notable improvement from previous productions. Opera as a contemporary art form is alive and kicking in Thailand.

MICHAEL PROUDFOOT

The Silent Prince (2016) European Tour

The performances of *The Silent Prince* in Bayreuth, Germany and in Prague and Brno in the Czech Republic were a breakthrough for international profile of Thai performance arts. Time and time again the reactions were not just praise for an exotic performance but an awed realization that Thailand should be treated, as an operatic entity, as a peer, not a curiosity.

For the first time, Europe began to realize that, in opera, Thailand has new things to say and has become a real, if still nascent, contributor to the medium.

Heavenly Gods and Devilishly Beautiful Women
German press review by Frank Piontek

BAYREUTH • *Nordbayerischer Kurier* • A celebration for the Queen. And a journey towards the genesis of *Parsifal*: the opera *The Silent Prince* both as narrative and as music, is a highlight of the Festival of Young Artists.

Even Queen Sirikit is, so to speak, present. In Thailand it is customary on this evening to celebrate her birthday, and so the Festival of Young Artists has placed a youthful portrait of the queen on the stage of the Europa Hall in the Zentrum where, just before the performance of "The Silent Prince", it will be with a candle procession.

The rite seems is honorable yet alien; but the Opera itself does not elevate monarchy per se. On the contrary, the mythical king in Somtow Sucharitkul's *Silent Prince,* who can not conceive why his son remains perpetually locked in a state of silent contemplation, is the most sinful figure of the evening. However, in the end he too shows himself to be "royal" in a different sense: the elevation of that same silent young man to *Bodhisattva*, the passive resistance against the temptations of power and love until the attainment of enlightenment — so, he aids in the redemption of his family and his people.

And that was ... *Parsifal*?

In the grand finale of the mainly diverting production, which brings us the heavenly gods as well as devilishly beautiful women from the enchanted gardens of the evil god Mara, we pay homage to the anointed Bodhisattva in an ecstatic, meditative tableau.

If you are not reminded of *Parsifal* in all this, you've never been to Bayreuth. The composer himself, in his notes, has explained how clearly he understands the links both to Wagner's *Bühnenweihfestspiel* and to the other grail opera *Lohengrin* — both as to the content and the musical relationships of his work. Yet in this new work, one sees no Wagnerian imitation. Indeed when one looks at the origin of certain ideas, it may have been more in a sense the other way round. For Richard Wagner himself who was studiously absorbed in the Buddhist myths and the Far Eastern world of ideas without his reading of that literature he could not have conceived *Tristan* or *Parsifal*. Sucharitkul is planning a ten-part cycle of Buddhist history; *The Silent Prince* is the first part — and it was enthusiastically received by the audience, because the composer truly understands his craft. This is a joyful and technically very accomplished syncretism. The stylistic collage conflates highly coloristic and saturated melodic lines with simple rhythms in the manner of the refined musical worlds of Franz Schreker (Vienna 1920), Leonard Bernstein and Steven Sondheim — combined with the sounds of his homeland. "Christian"-sounding organ chords are played against the buzzing sounds of sitar; Western tonalities are overlaid with

Southeast Asian melodies. But rather than creating a confused chaos of sound, Sucharitkul has fashioned an exciting score in which - and this is what is so modern about it - East and West are united in harmony yet with their differences clearly audible —partaking fully in the spirit of this festival.

Free Will and Pre-destination

And the subject matter of this work? The ancient Buddhist myths have enlightened Europeans concerning the interplay of free will and determinism. This tale of morality and obstinacy has something to tell us today. The idea of "enlightenment" seems esoteric at first glance. yet to pit peace of mind against the chatter and the corruption of this world is a viable alternative view.

The performance sparkles with a powerful chamber orchestra conducted by Trisdee Na Patalung, a small but excellent choir, the impressive high soprano Queen of Heaven Nadlada Thamtanakom, Colleen Brooks as the Queen of Kashi and the equally high soprano of the Prince, who is silent for two hours until the very end, when in a massive final aria, he sings the most of all: Jak Cholvijarn is this young man who not only makes one forget his long motionlessness in this *Bühnenweihfestspiel*, but whose performance even justifies the precending period of quietness.

A massive round of applause for both an opera that is both scenically alien — yet musically accessible — whose music soars high and even as its ethics plumb depths of profundity.

Commentary from the Czech media

from *Opera +*, the leading Czech classical music magazine • by David Chaloupka

With little fanfare during a rather operatically deprived summer in the capital city of Prague, in the Palac Akropolis was played a historic first Thai premier opera on Czech territory. By no means, however, was this just an ethnographical curiosity of an evening, but an extremely professional display of contemporary Thai culture in a fusion with European operatic structure.

The opera *The Silent Prince* was created by Thai composer Somtow Sucharitkul five years ago as a result of a commission from the Opera Vista, a small opera company in Houston, Texas. As the composer himself wittily explained before the show, the only condition of the contract was the story be set in India, as it was funded by a grant from the Indian community in Houston.

Renowned Thai composer and writer (in the genre of science fiction and horror literature) **Somtow Sucharitkul** (born in 1952) chose one of the oldest Buddhist subjects. *The Silent Prince* is based on the Buddhist principle of reincarnation. The Buddha was reincarnated many times before reaching Buddha-hood and this story is about his youth in one of those reincarnations. It is a surprising and interesting choice of subject, but some of the composer's other operas such as *Madana*, *Mae Naak* and *Ayodhya* are also based on traditional Thai and Buddhist themes.

The opera is in a prologue and five scenes (a total of about 100 minutes) draws from a well-known Buddhist legend about the prince, who was born in the royal palace in Benares. Prince Temiya (a name derived by the time of his birth, the season of the monsoon) ceases to speak when told to give the order to execute a condemned criminal. At that moment of decision he sees a vision of the evil perpetuated in previous lives. The royal parents, and the court try desperately, but the young man remains mute. The father then orders his servant to take him into the forest and kill him. When digging the grave in a clearing, an unearthly light shines from the depths.

Prince Temiya appears in the form of a divine Bodhisattva. Everyone, including parents coming in it recognize the divine incarnation and the opera ends with the live image of deities and humans.

Although the plot may seem like a fairytale, the story line comes to vivid life with the appearances of Buddhist deities and scenes of paradise or the underworld. The opera carries a timeless message, which, as regards the principle of reincarnation, but has also a strong relationship to mankind today. Everything we've ever done and decided to remain in our soul indelibly imprinted. Composer, then in the beginning also said that he was fascinated by the subject because of parallels with the fate of children affected by autism or post-traumatic loss of speech. Moreover, he attracted the paradox that in an opera, in which the voice is a fundamental means of expression, the title character could remain mute until the final scene. I hope he knows Auber's opera *La Muette De Portici*, in which similar theatrical effect is achieved.

The performing touring ensemble has economical "travel" solution - a single scene, a small choir, six dancers. But it is a thoroughly professional ensemble, and before Prague the work has already premiered in Germany. Above all, it is necessary to appreciate the performance of twenty-five piece orchestra, bringing to life the colorful and exotic score with excellent conducting. The music has very accessible, neo-

romantic character, with occasional touches of sober modernist expression and sound. The composer includes light hints of local rhythms and local tonalities. The music is not derivative, even though we hear processes and solutions that we find in the works of Benjamin Britten for example, and some sweet tunes (especially in the women's roles) reminding one of the musicals of Andrew Lloyd Webber. The composition is scored for a traditional orchestra, accompanied by several instruments of Southeast Asian Nations (tambura) and other onomatopoeic effects are realized electronically.

Design: wonderfully colorful and ornate costumes (which was their bright colors carry other meanings) choreography and performances based on traditional Southeast Asian aesthetics, but subtly adapted to the comprehensibility of a western audience.

The opera is carried primarily by the two major party royal parents. German baritone **Falko Honisch**, a well known oratorio singer and operatic who has sung roles from Wagner to baroque music, and American mezzo-soprano **Colleen Brooks,** who works primarily in the US, for example in roles such as Rossini, with roles advised well, despite some problems with higher tones at high soprano and initial intonation issues with the baritone.

The greatest attention was drawn to coloratura soprano **Nadlada Thamtanakom** whose attrractive and flexible soprano created three roles - the Queen of Heaven, the goddess of illusion Maya and courtesans, the role to which the composer put a lot of decorative singing whose difficulty resemble places parts of the Queen of the Night and Christina from the musical *Phantom of the Opera*.

Prince Temiya (the character is represented by a little boy and then an adult singer, who until the very end of the opera is silent), thus its subsequent divine form, is played by counter-tenor (**Jak Cholvijarn**), whose vocal sexless character perfectly corresponds with the ethereal essence. His duet with Sunanda, the king's aide (proficient tenor **Kittin Suchato**), who has to execute the sentence of the prince, then reminds us of the scene between Apollo and Aschenbach of Britten's *Death in Venice*.

Ten Lives of the Buddha Preview (2016)

In a special performance to mark the creation of the first four works in the *DasJati* sequence and a sneak preview of excerpts from upcoming episodes, Opera Siam presented scenes from several of the *DasJati* compositions. The production was blessed with the appearance of Khun Ploypailin Jensen as the goddess Atman — the soul of humanity.

left:

post-rehearsal notes with cast including K Ployparilin Jensen

below:

grand finale of *Bhuridat* sequence with nagas, elephamys and cast

Khun Ploypailin Jensen as the goddess of the soul onstage, and below, with team from Thai Bev, husband David, Somtow and producer Thaithow, and Deputy Director of the Department of Cultural Promotion

Chariot of Heaven (2017)

    The fourth of the DasJati stories concerns King Nemiraj, a personage of such supreme goodness that he is invited to heaven to preach to the thirty-three gods of the Tavatimsa Heaven.

    On his way to heaven he visits hell and choreographer Puwarate created a strangely erotic yet horrifying vision that included souls imprisoned in tiny cages, climbing poles, and trying to devour each other.

    The scene in heaven provided an opportunity for something that has never been done in an opera. Because the thirty-three gods of Tavatimsa are named characters in Buddhist cosmology, Somtow decided to create an ensemble of thirty-three separate voices for it. Musically this tour-de-force had never been attempted and performing it in Thailand made the Thailand Cultural Center the scene of another "first" in the history of music.

Trisdee na Patalung, the resident conductor of Opera Siam, intent as he directs a scene from *Chariot of Heaven*. Below: the gates of hell open up for King Nemi

Bangkok Post

reviewed by Sirilaksana Khoman

Somtow Sucharitkul's world premiere of his latest production in the Dasjati series, Nemiraj: Chariot of Heaven, is a sumptuous feast for the senses. Aptly chosen to commemorate the 100th day since the passing of our beloved King Bhumibol Adulyadej, it embodies profound spiritual thought, deep introspection and great beauty.

The Dasjati are the last 10 of the Jataka tales which literally mean 'birth history', a voluminous body of literature about the lives of the Buddha. In the complete Jataka, these lives take on animal as well as human form, ranging from king, outcast, god, tortoise, fish, elephant, and other animals — each didactic story succinctly conveying moral lessons or principles. The Jataka can be likened to fables or spiritual parables, pedagogical tools that rely on analogy to illustrate and impart some virtue, making use of humble incidents to teach great truths. The animal forms underscore the philosophy that all life is sacred, discouraging the tendency towards anthropocentrism in which humans dominate and control other forms of life.

The last ten lives (Tosachart, in Thai), are being portrayed most exquisitely by Somtow Sucharitkul in his Dasjati ballet-opera series.

This latest installment, Nemiraj, is visually pleasing and vividly imaginative, especially in its varied musical color. As a musical feast, it is simply delicious. The orchestra, conducted by Trisdee Na Patalung, played Somtow's delightful score with élan and sensitivity. The interesting mix of Asian and Western tones, replete with Indian tanpura, Russian theremin, Thai flute (pi java), French celesta, blending in with the standard orchestral pieces, demonstrates how captivatingly expressive this music can be. Our perceptions are awakened and challenged. And particularly moving, are the sounds familiar to all Thais, that herald the King's arrival or departure.

The orchestra's impeccable phrasing provided an ideal texture to complement the soloists and not overwhelm them, and the singing performances were stellar. As Matali, guiding the celestial chariot, Camp Asawa may have given his most memorable performance to date.

Overall the production was well-cast, showcasing the vocal and dramatic prowess of the soloists, the Siam Orpheus Choir and the supporting Immanuel Lutheran Children's Choir. The dancers exhibited energy and polish, and the staging was luscious, with décor and costumes to match. It would be remiss not to mention the clear libretto and the delectable translations by Khun Thaithow Sucharitkul, capturing the marvelous tale of profound meditation on life and death, good and evil, the choice between giving alms and charity as opposed to meditation and prayer, seeking a lofty ataraxia, striving to achieve "Sunyata" (or emptiness) since both good and evil are perceived as part of an antagonistic duality that itself must be overcome.

In 1919, Irish poet W. B. Yeats described his world as one in which the "best lack all conviction, while the worst are full of passionate intensity". Works of art depicting or exploring spiritual development, morality and ethical introspection are clearly important in generating discussion and fostering that "conviction", particularly in an age where isolationism, prejudice, and even bigotry and racism are blatantly preached. Spiritual development cuts across creed and colour, and only through open discussion, engagement and open-mindedness, through the arts and other media, can we hope to uplift our consciousness and stem the rising tide of intolerance.

Heaven, Earth and Hell in *Nemiraj: Chariot of Heaven*

Sama: The Faithful Son (2015)
Bangkok Premiere

After its premiere at the remarkable Suryadhep in Rangsit University, *The Faithful Son* had its Bangkok premiere two years later. The stellar cast returned. Cassandra

Black, as the statue of Bahusodari, was a particular audience favorite.

The larger stage and ability to use trap doors and lifts allowed some extra bits of stagecraft.

Stacey Tappan, the much loved soprano who is a regular performer at the Met in New York, was a new member of the cast in this incarnation of *The Faithful Son.*

Cassandra Black speaks about *DasJati*

The statue moves! *is an unforgettable moment from the third chapter of the ten-part* **DasJati** *series of music dramas. Cassandra Black, American dramatic soprano who created the role, shares her thoughts about it. Sitting in her Houston home as the floodwaters have been rising, Cassandra contributed her insights to the* **DasJati** *newsletter.*

One never forgets the first time one meets Somtow Sucharitkul. I'd had the honor of singing for a wonderful conductor, Viswa Subbaraman, for a few years when he called me and said, "A great composer I know is casting a dramatic soprano for a world premiere he's working on called *The Snow Dragon*. Would you be interested?"

Having some experience with twentieth century composers I was very keen and the idea of playing a dragon was beyond exciting! I remember getting the score and being so moved by how Somtow treated the subject matter, the orchestration, and the melody in a fantasy world I'd never yet dreamed of; one could swim in it! The role was a perfect fit. From the costume to the plot, the staging to the gorgeous music, it was a conscience dream.

On the opening weekend Somtow came to see the show. I was fascinated by this person who seemed to have lived ten lives, himself. Never had I met such a renaissance man; he was about as quirky and strange as you might imagine any genius to be. It was love at first sight. About a year later I was presented with the opportunity to be involved with *Das Jati* and I couldn't believe my good fortune.

The role of the Statue in *Suwana Sama* comes to life to sing her demanding aria about two thirds of the way through the show. While Somtow was writing it he presented the easy-way-out where upon the company would create a statue of me and, with smoke and mirrors, switch me out for my sculpture double at some point so I wouldn't have to remain immobile for so long. Who doesn't want a life-sized statue of one's self?! As any performer knows, it's much harder to stand still on stage than to be moving!

But there's one thing Somtow and I have always seen eye to eye on: drama. I knew that if I could be still for that long, the moment the statue came to life would be truly magical. I offered to be the statue the whole show.

Never has a role been more physically demanding. I prepared by going to *Wats* every day to practice stillness, at first five minutes, building to an hour and a half. As a westerner, meditation came to mean something else to me entirely. After sitting still in the make-up chair for two hours before the role, there is something almost religious in the experience every night that no other role has ever done for me.

As of now I am three days into the massive event known as Hurricane Harvey. Houston, home of 7-9 million people, my current home, and the home of the first performance of *Das Jati* is under the third constant day of flooding. We have now started controlled releasing of our dams, flooding hundreds of homes to save thousands. Zilkha Hall, where *Das Jati* was first performed is tragically under water. Like Opera Siam, I have faith that Houston will hold together and live to dream another day. Houston and Bangkok are not so different in that our size has never made us less of a community.

Thailand has a true hold on my heart. I cannot put it in words. My experiences there have been a daily salve on my thirst for life. The country has taught me stillness within chaos, excitement within monotony, and true friendship with those from the other side of the globe. I tear up every time I say goodbye to her and feel something missing in myself when I'm away from her. The language, the pace, and most of all the people have become a part of who I am at my core. And it all started with a wonderful conductor introducing me to the maker of the *Snow Dragon*.

BANGKOK -- *You cannot really get upset when Somtow Sucharitkul arrives more than 30 minutes late for an interview. His excuse is hard to beat. Deeply immersed in another world -- of gods, demons and holy men -- Thailand's "Renaissance man" was composing a scene from what is shaping into arguably the largest integrated work in classical music -- ever.*

By 2020 -- "If I am still around," he jokes - Somtow, now 63, will have completed a cycle of 10 operas based on the Jataka tales, stories popular across Asia which depict the previous lives of Gautama Buddha. In duration, at least, the work will have surpassed that Mount Everest of opera, the 19th century *Der Ring des Nibelungen*by Richard Wagner, which clocks in at around 16 hours for the four operas.

DasJati, as Somtow calls the cycle, has been described by Britain's Opera Now magazine as "the most extended music drama of all time," while the already performed works of the opus have drawn consistently positive reviews. *Mahosat*, an epic of war and deliverance and the sixth opera of the cycle, will be ready for staging next year.

To risk stereotyping, something Somtow himself confronts from time to time, one might not expect an Asian composer to rise to the forefront of contemporary opera, Western-style. But Somtow has long defied cultural pigeonholing and being restricted to any one creative endeavor, or geography.

Somtow Sucharitkul first gained international recognition as an author of fantasy, science fiction and horror novels, including cult classics "Vampire Junction." (Photo by Denis Gray)

Born into a royal Thai family, educated at England's Eton College and Cambridge University, he spent much of his life in the U.S. Although steeped in music from an early age -- he composed his first opera as a schoolboy -- Somtow gained international recognition as an author of fantasy, science fiction and horror novels. His more than 50 books have sold over 2 million copies worldwide. Some, like

"Vampire Junction," are established cult classics. While living near Hollywood, he even tried his hand at movie directing. "The kills are gruesome and inventive, a fun ride," wrote one critic of his work "The Laughing Dead."

First love

After an earlier stint in his homeland, Somtow returned to Thailand permanently in 2001 and to his first love, throwing himself into a maelstrom of musical composition and performance. Somtow also founded the Siam Philharmonic, which he frequently conducts, an award-winning youth orchestra and the Opera Siam company, establishing Bangkok as the opera hub of Southeast Asia and enhancing the once lackluster classical music scene.

"When I had the vision of creating an opera company I didn't really know we would be starting from absolute scratch -- no funding, no built-in audience, an orchestra that couldn't play this kind of music," he said. "I started a whole movement. I think this will be a greater artistic contribution than any of the music or books I have written," he notes.

Somtow conducts the Siam Philharmonic Orchestra in a performance of Beethoven's 9th Symphony. (Courtesy of Puriwat Charoenying).

Somtow's compositions -- symphonies, ballets, operas and two requiems, including one in memory of the World Trade Center attack victims -- have been described as a synthesis of Western neo-Romantic and neo-Asian idioms. A Somtow piece, for example, may include a harpsichord and a *renad*, or traditional Thai xylophone. His opera stagings often transpose original settings to Asia: the Egypt of Verdi's Aida becomes the ancient Thai kingdom of Ayuthaya, a *tuk-tuk* features in Mozart's The Magic Flute and Wagner's killer dragon Fafner appears in the shape of a giant crane during Bangkok's building boom.

But some of his musical horizons have nothing to do with Asia. For example, Somtow believes he has a "strange connection" with the Holocaust which he cannot explain, and for three years has been struggling to finish a "very dark" opera about a Jewish woman who carried on a passionate affair with a Nazi guard at the Auschwitz concentration camp.

A scene from The Silent Prince, the first opera of Somtow's cycle which was premiered in the U.S. (Courtesy of Puriwat Charoenying)

"I refuse to commit myself to an ethnic identity of any kind, which necessarily narrows me as a person and makes me less human," he said.

Before Somtow's arrived on the scene, Bangkok was already beginning to absorb Western classical music. The Bangkok Symphony Orchestra was born in 1982, and five years later the 2,000-seat, Japanese-funded Thailand Cultural Center opened its doors. World class artists started to include Bangkok on their tours.

from the Prague premiere of *The Silent Prince*

New trajectory

With his high-profile projects, Somtow unquestionably set the Thai capital on a new musical trajectory. He is often asked by Thai journalists why he "does all this foreign stuff."

"My answer is: 'Are you saying we should give up TV and the movies? These are all foreign art forms. And that we should only have *likay*(traditional Thai folktheater)?'" Somtow told the Nikkei Asian Review. "This classical music is like a huge inheritance that we have received. We are not re-creating Europe in Asia. We may be beginning with this raw material which we have inherited, but we are putting our own stamp on. We are creating our own thing with it."

While other Asian capitals may enjoy greater funding for the arts, Somtow says they have tended to continue a post-colonial trend in emulating second-rate European opera houses whereas Bangkok generated a "wild and adventurous vision."

The fifth opera of Somtow's cycle, Nemiraj, is a work of epic proportions, musically and story-wise. (Courtesy of Puriwat Charoenying)

Somtow's Jataka cycle awaits critical appraisal -- a festival of all 10 operas is planned for 2020 -- but it is without doubt highly adventurous. Some of its operas are intimate -- the first, *The Silent Prince*, scored for only 20 instruments. Others are massive in scale, spanning eons and involving hundreds of characters. The fifth, Nemiraj, boasts another operatic first: an ensemble with individual vocal lines for 33 soloists, representing 33 deities, described as a "harmonic tsunami" using only three chords stretched out over eight minutes.

Writing *The Silent Prince* on a commission for Opera Vista, in Houston, Texas, Somtow says it was only while in the middle of working on a third opera based on the Jataka tales -- a Harry Potter-like story of magic and wizardry -- that he conceived of an entire cycle. "When this happened I thought, 'Nah, this is ridiculous. We already have the Ring,'" he said. "But it was an idea which just wouldn't let go. The seeds of the whole cycle are all planted. I suppose I am now essentially watering them."

Somtow recently took his company to Bayreuth, the German town sacred to Wagnerians. During the celebrated annual festival of Wagner's works there, he did a "very cheeky" thing. On an off-night, Somtow invited festival attendees to a staging of *The Silent Prince* in a small auditorium.

The reception, by audience and critics, proved extremely favorable, and was even better in the Czech Republic, where some critics expressed amazement that this was "a real opera, not just an ethnographic display."

"When Asian performing artists go to Europe they are treated rather like performing monkeys: 'Oh, how sweet that you guys can play our music,'" Somtow said. "I think what was really gratifying was being treated as a peer ensemble."

How did you become involved in the "DasJati project"?

Henry Akina, the General Director for the Hawai'i Opera Theatre first asked me to collaborate with him as a scenic designer for the Bangkok Opera's production of Madama Butterfly in 2007. Henry's vision was to create a striking but simple environment of "light and shadows" to express time and place in the story. Upon my arrival at the first rehearsal, I was struck with the world class talent that Somtow had managed to assemble and was gratified to hear positive feedback from these veteran performers about the set. Henry submitted this idea as the genesis of what would become the most successful production of "Butterfly" at the prestigious Savonlinna Opera Festival in Finland with an unprecedented 4 reprises.

Many years later, as I was launching a 2.0 version of the San Francisco Lyric Opera as its Executive Director, I was surprised to hear from Thaithow Sucharitkul to design the sets for The Nation's Reya the Musical based on her book "Reya". After a fantastic run, Somtow then asked me about designing the set for "The Silent Prince", the first installment of DasJati, a series of performances chronicling the 10 lives of Buddha. It was an extremely rewarding experience and one that I must admit helped me through a very serious health crisis I was having at the time.

Are you influenced by Buddhist philosophy or Asian aesthetics in your designs for DasJati? Did you know the stories beforehand?

I have always had an affinity for Asian design and have been fascinated at how much influence the arts of Asia had on many of the European masters from the 19th century onward. I feel that it was this influence that Henry Akina and I proposed to Savonlinna that got us the commission. However, the weight of tackling this effort after realizing that there are probably thousands of visual representations of these stories painted or carved on temple walls all over Asia made me realize that this was actually a historic undertaking. As an Japanese American Christian whose grandparents had a portrait of Jesus and the Lambs hung on the wall along with Buddhist and Shinto shrines in the living room, my exposure to Buddhism was rather diluted! However, going to Buddhist temples as a child for family occasions exposed me to Buddhism as more of a philosophy than a religion. Some of these stories seem familiar but I did not have the structure of a formal education. I have, however also visited sites in Japan, China, Thailand and Indonesia where I have seen some of these stories depicted in their artwork.

Working in Thailand is challenging for many people. What were some of your experiences?

Growing up in Hawai'i, I learned quickly that I had to adjust the way I interacted with people when I moved to the US Mainland for college. Actually, I have learned that Hawaiians and Thais have a very similar outlook on interpersonal relations and that helped me navigate the nuances

Dean Shibuya speaks about *DasJati*

and complexities of Thai culture. Working in Bangkok seems like a natural fit for me as a result, but I can understand how challenging it can be for someone with a more "western" work ethic.

You've run the San Francisco Lyric Opera and other organizations in the west. How different is the approach?

Generally, in the US there is a more entrenched culture of philanthropy and, as government funding has fallen, private donor support has become even more important. As one can imagine, competition has increased because of this and fundraising comprises a huge part of the operating budget. Events are planned to announce seasons and donor appreciation parties are a necessity. At the Lyric, we also offered individual "Producer" credit for persons who donate for a specific production in return for access to rehearsals and dress rehearsals. On the production side, I think that the main difference is the amount of rehearsal time we were allowed in a space. At the Thailand Cultural center, we are lucky to have two full days prior to opening night. The lighting and costume designers as well as the stage crew have been a dream to work with.

The DasJati project was on hold for almost two years while Somtow struggled with health issues and Thailand was plunged into mourning because of the passing of King Rama IX. Do you think other delays are likely, and do you believe the project will be completed?

I hope not. If a season is announced and has to be adjusted at the last minute for whatever reason, it would make a potential subscriber or donor very reticent to purchase a ticket beyond an upcoming performance. This perpetuates the hand to mouth existence of the company. Having a strong long term cash flow program is absolutely required to be able to plan with confidence. In addition, a Planned Giving Program would inject some additional resources in the future to add to an endowment to help stabilize of the day to day operating expenses.

Do you think you've become "more Asian" because of this project?

My involvement with Opera Siam and particularly my work with several of the DasJati operas has been so fulfilling as a designer in so many ways. One of them is indeed my own self identity as a person of Asian (Japanese) descent. Being an Asian American born and raised in Hawai'I, I believe I had the unique perspective of growing up in an environment that was considered a "melting pot" of different (mostly Asian) races and cultures. That said, while researching the history and architecture for DaJati , as well as absorbing its lessons and mores, I have discovered that my own personal connection with my identity as Asian has been strengthened.

What is your approach to the DasJati series when it comes to design? What are you trying to say?

My approach as a designer for DasJati series is to convey a sense of history and location but with a timeless quality . Blending history and mythology can be tricky and I have tried to be careful in not inserting too many literal design elements into the sets. However, using design vocabulary from locations that these tales take place is an effective way of conveying the appropriate context to the story telling. I also like to use lighting as a major tool in creating an environment and my designs always consider how lighting itself can become a "character" as well.

Coasting to Enlightenment (2018)

By 2017, five of the ten episodes of *DasJati* had been composed and had been produced on stage. *The Silent Prince* had been seen in two different productions in the USA and in Europe — with astonishingly positive reviews.

Other excerpts from *DasJati* had been heard around the world — a suite with music from all the works up to that time, for instance, was performed with much success all over the south of Germany.

It looked as though we were on track to do the entire series by 2020.

The passing of His Majesty King Rama IX was a tragedy that also affected the productions; our team was occupied in putting together events such as *48 Forever,* the first symphonic concerts of the entire oeuvre of His Majesty King Rama IX.

However, in 2018, no new episode of *DasJati* was produced as composer Somtow spent more than two years composing one of the most spectacular works in the sequence, *Mahosot — Architect of Dreams.*

However, the year was not completely devoid of *DasJati.*

In its second visit to Carnegie Hall, the Siam Sinfonietta had played an excerpt from *Bhuridat* and in its third, in 2018, the Sinfonietta did the sneak preview of the *Magic Palace* scene from *Architect of Dreams.* Like the *Dragon Dance* previously, this was greeted with a standing ovation.

With numerous stress-causing events during the hiatus, progress on the composition of this monumental work suffered, But Somtow managed to produce the fifth and seventh works in the sequence and they were both in June, 2019 ... bringing the total number of produced works in the sequence to seven.

The remaining works now all exist in sketch form and Opera Siam has decided that it will produce the largest work of all, the mighty Tenth Jataka, *Prince Vessantara,* during 2020. This is the work perhaps most looked-forward to by the local audience as it is he most popular of the jataka tales.

The 8th and 9th works are smaller, chamber-sized works and are designed ultimately to be performed alongside the 7th in a triptych, allowing the ten music dramas to be done during the course of five evenings.

The current plan is therefore now to do a major production of *Prince Vessantara* at the beginning of August, 2020, a time close to the birthday of the Tenth Rama — auspicious for the performance of the Tenth Jataka.

Architect of Dreams
(2019)

Mahosahda - Architect of Dreams had the longest composition time of the seven thus far produced, as parts of it were written as early as 2016 and the last notes were not done until 2019. The original text is one of the most baroquely picaresque of the jatakas, telling the tale of a merchant's son who is a kind of "universal genius", able to solve problems, create palaces out of thin air, pass learned judgments, and becomes the chief advisor to a foolish but well-meaning King, Vedeha, who previously has been unduly influenced by four corrupt advisors.

Clockwise from left:

Pop Chaiportn as the insouciant King Vedeha; Dag Schantz as King Julani, who is trying to conquer the world; Damian Whiteley as the cunning Kevatta; and Sassaya Chavalit as Princess Panjalajandi with her pet mynah bird, Mintra Manchakra. Elizabeth Moran as the parrot.

During the course of this opera, young Mahosadha singlehandedly defeats one hundred and one enemy armies, delivers a Solomon-like judgment to two squabbling mothers, builds a huge palace in a single night, abducts the daughter of the kingdom's enemy and acts as matchmaker between her and his King ... all the while besting the palace's wily politicians and kibbitzing with his pet parrot (who seduced a mynah bird in their enemy's palace.) It is a busy opera.

Of the ten tales in DasJati, *Architect of Dreams* is the one closest to all-out comedy. The musical writing focuses on flashes of bright color with many exotic effects. Only in Panjalajandi's poignat aria *Lonely am I* does the music paint a more tranquil, more lyrical picture. Of the ten works, this one is perhaps the most technically difficult for the orchestra.

Chandakumar (2019)

The seventh of the Ten *DasJati* was premiered in June if 2019 as part of a double bill along with *Mahosot: Architect of Dreams.*

Since the Pali text is only a few pages long for this tale, Somtow decided to create a vignette, thirty minutes long, which is a ballet inside a framing mini-opera. The story of a king who has a dream of heaven, and is then told by an evil counsellor that to attain this heaven he must sacrifice four each of the most precious things in the kingdom.

The plot's true purpose is to murder the King's son, Chandakumar, who is actually a Bodhisattva, and whose sagacity and learned judgments are a threat to Kandahala, the wicked advisor.

Taken in by the counsellor, King Ekaraja prepares a sacrifical ceremony and is about to kill all the innocent victims when Chandakumar begins a highly concentrated meditation, so focused and concentrated that he is able to manifest the Divine Principle of Shakro Devanam Indra, ruler of the Heaven of Thirty-three.

Indra disposes of Ekaraja's trappings of kingship, frees the captives, destroys the sacrificial idol, and anoints Chandakumar as the new king of Puppavati.

The opera-ballet is accompanied by an orchestra consisting entirely of fours: four stringed instruments, four woodwinds, four brass, four percussionists, and four struck and plucked instruments, representing the sets of four sacriicial victims of each category.

The unusual orchestral sound world is one of extremely transparent colorations and virtuoso playing from all the participants.

The seventh, eighth and ninth works in the series are designed as a triptych, each accompanied by a different chamber orchestra, as an interlude between the large and fantastical *Bhuridat* and the large-scale finale, *Prince Vessantara* which celebrates the Bodhisattva's final step in his journey to Buddha-hood.

Above: crushing the idol, Indra leads a group of divine beings to free the city of Puppavati from the tyrant Ekaraja.

Right: The Bodhisattva meditates

Below: celestial beings dance and sing in Ekaraja's dream of heaven

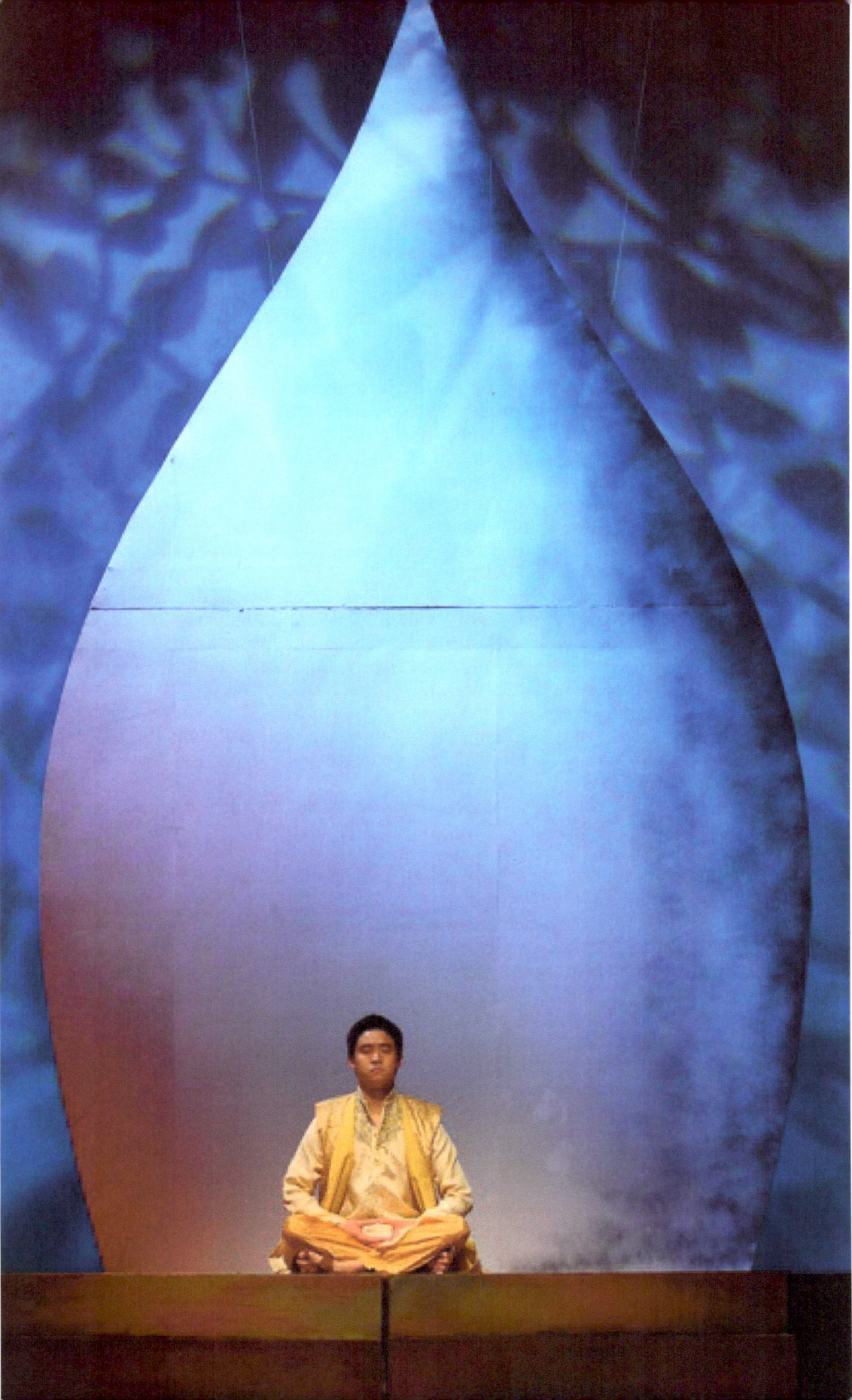

The European Cultural Achievement Award 2017
Acceptance Speech

Your Excellencies, Ladies and Gentlemen:

Mr. Topp, the president of the European Culture Forum, has painted a glowing picture of my achievements. I will be long dead before we find out if history will validate his praise.

But, as the first winner of the European Cultural Achievement Award to come from a place once quaintly known as "The Far East", I feel that the award is less about what I have done, but about how far WE have come, as a nation, as a region, in taking our rightful seat at the table of the world's culture.

When I was a child growing up many European countries, I would sometimes see performances from Thai or other Asian artists. I could sense that though these performances were greeted with respect and interest, there was always a sense that what we did was something *other,* outside the mainstream. "How charming! These clever little natives are playing our music!"

But in only the last few years, there has been an absolute and permanent change in how the world views us. When this orchestra, created using a radical educational theory, became the first Thai symphony orchestra to win the first prize in any major international competition, five years ago, interpreting the music of Austria to a panel consisting entirely of Austrian judges, the foreman of the jury said, "We have heard the message from the young people of Thailand. We have heard it loud and clear." Last year, when part of my DasJati series toured in Europe, a Czech reviewer said, "This was by no means an ethnographical curiosity, but a fully professional display of contemporary Thai culture in fusion with European traditions."

There was a time when the west saw us as unformed, as pristine vessels ready to receive western culture as a divine gift. But those days are over. The west has come to understand that our relationship is no longer only about what can learn; it is now equally about what we can teach.

There are many people who have made today possible, and I would like to thank some of them who are in this hall.

I would like to thank my family, who defied the conventions of society by allowing me the freedom to follow a different road, illumined by a different light.

Many countries have welcomed me and let my voice be heard. In particular, tonight I thank Germany, represented this evening by Dr. Prügel, the ambassador the first European country to embrace my work.

I would like to mention some of the educational institutions of this country, who have tolerated my out-of-the-box methods and allowed my holistic approach to flourish. In particular, I would like to mention Dr. Arthit Ourairat, whose visionary approach has conjured up a new performing arts center where once there was nothing, appearing like a magical oasis in a suburban desert.

And I would like to thank my fellow artists, who have been with me on this thrilling journey. It's been a hard journey.

But we have come to understand that we too are participants in the great drama of the world. That we too may stand on the stages of the world and show its audiences truths that they would have remained unseen, had we not been there to show them. Whether it is in theater, film, the visual arts, dance, or, now, in classical music, the artists of Thailand now dare to hold up the mirror to the world.

We have inherited many great forms of expression from western culture — among them film, television, and opera. But these gifts are no longer shiny trinkets from another land. They are our inheritance. They belong to us, and we have new things to say about them.

We may now dare to show the audiences of the world who they are, because we have finally dared to understand who we are.

As to the question of who we are, I would like to draw your attention to the quintessentially Thai thing I know. This is not some architectural marvel, or some arcane dance, but something ubiquitous, and known throughout the world: the simple Thai salad, or *yam*.

This is the most amazing invention. The great secret of *yam* is that every ingredient retains its original texture, its original identity. And yet, this dish has a gestalt that is unmistakably Thai in every bite.

Our culture is like that salad. There's a nibble of India, a crunch of China, a sprinkle of Hollywood, and you can see all the pieces, each disparate, each unique. But the whole thing could never be anything other than Thai.

This is the culture that transformed a pile of broken pottery into the Temple of Dawn.

In this regard, I am so happy the cultural world is beginning to notice what I'm trying to do in creating the *DasJati* series. Of course a lot of people are hung up on its 'giganticism' — you see a lot of commentators mentioning it's the "biggest integrated work of classical music in history" and that sort of thing.

But the canvas needs to be big, because the strands being woven together are so multitudinous and so diverse. Buddhism as music drama, told in a language drawn as much from film as from theater and in a musical idiom that bridges Europe and Asia; it's not just the story of a religion, but a story about all of us, the people in today's world.

It's a project that will bring together creative individuals from many fields, and which, I hope, can be interpreted and reinterpreted by the ever-widening viewpoints of future artists.

Since returning to Thailand almost two decades ago after several decades of searching for identity and meaning, I've learned a simple truth that is difficult to learn; that home is not a place, but a feeling; that to know the world you must first dare to know yourself.

It is therefore as a Thai artist, and in the name of Thailand's many great artists on whose shoulders I stand, and on behalf of this great country that has brought me to this moment, that I accept, with humility, the 2017 Award for European Cultural Achievement.

The Ten Music Dramas as they unfold

1 • Temiya • The Silent Prince
a chamber opera

first produced by Opera Vista, Houston, Texas in 2010; subsequent productions Bangkok 2012, 2013; Bayreuth, Prague, Brno, 2016

scored for a chamber orchestra with double string quartet and solo winds

2 • Mahajanaka • The Ocean of Dharma
an oratorio-ballet

originally *Mahajanaka Symphony* composed in 1996 as part of HM King Rama IX fifth cycle jubilee celebrations. Adapted into a stage work in 2014 with additional music and transitions.

scored for symphony orchestra with large chorus and soprano soloist in the role of the goddess Meghala.

3 • Sama • The Faithful Son

first produced in 2015 at Rangsit University's Suryadhep Hall; revived in Bangkok 2017.

scored for two chamber orchestras, on either side of the conductor, representing the constantly shifting dualities of the story

4 • Nemiraj • Chariot of Heaven
opera with dance episodes

first produced in Bangkok in 2017 on the 100-day-memorial for the passing of H.M. King Rama IX; the opera describes the journey of King Nemi through 84,000 generations, and through heaven and hell

unusual features include the use of extreme pitches in orchestration representing the extremes of the human condition, a prominent role for a theremin, and the ensemble number of 33 discrete soloists representing the 33 gods of the Tavatimsa Heaven

5 • Mahosot • Architect of Dreams
comic opera

premiered in Bangkok in 2019, this picaresque comedy is characterised by a plethora of colorations and lightning-fast harmonic shifts; orchestrated for a large symphony orchestra. Some sounds, iike the use of sistrum, unique to this work in the series. Excerpts previewed by the Siam Sinfonietta during its Carnegie Hall tour, 2018.

6 • Bhuridat • The Dragon Lord
opera with dance episodes

first performed in Thailand in 2014, this production featured aerial ballet representing an epic battle between a garuda and a naga, and the "dragon dance" performed by the Bodhisattva while under the spell of the evil Alambayana.

This score is colored with the use of the "pi java" — the Thai war-oboe as symbol of magic, as well as by several exotic ballet numbers that have been played as a suite.

7 • Chandakumar • The Sacrifice

This brief vignette tells the story of how Prince Chandakumar prevents his deluded father from sacrificing four of each of the most valuable creatures in his Kingdom — including his wives and sons.

The narrative of this work is a mini-ballet framed within a mini-opera. The orchestra consists of sets of four soloists: four strings, four woodwinds, four brass, four percussionists, and four hammered/plucked instruments.

Not yet produced: *8 • Narada • The Great Brahma* — *9 • Vidhura • The True Heart* — and *10 • Vessantara • The Supreme Gift*

DAS·JATI

Charter Members of the DasJati Project

These members have pledged to make an annual contribution to the project for five years.

Mahadeva (200,000)
Thai Yarnyon Co., Ltd.
Dr. Arthit Ourairat
Dr. Nadaprapai Sucharitkul
Pisit Laosirirat
Prayuth Mahagitsiri
Dr. Sompong Sucharitkul
Yos Euarchukiati

Akkradeva (100,000)
Institute of Metropolitan
    Development (Mahakorn 3)
Christian Ham
Piyabutr Cholvijarn
Santi Pranich

Deva (50,000)
Somtow Sucharitkul
Dr. Thanat Khoman and Family
Anonymous
Anyonymous

Mahadevi (20,000)
Studio 28
Suichart Dej-Udom

Devi (10,000)
Anonymous
Karen Schur-Narula
Michael Proudfoot
Preecha Udomkijdecha
Raksak Kananurak
Suchart Milsted
Tom Page
Donald Moisen
Janneke Bomhoff

Apsara (5,000)
Chaiporn Chinaprayoon
Chongkonnee Wongpashukchot
Gerard Isaacson
Lesley D. Junlakan
Linda Cummings
Orapin Kanchanagorn
Patrick Drnec
Sakda Lormsomboon
Sirikarn Luengvarintra
Sunetra Rasmussen
Ted and Jeanne Shibuya
Thidaporn Sermchai
Michael Khandelwal
Susan Kepner

Apsarini (2,000)
Bjorn Lindstrom
Choopong Kiangsiri
Dag Johanessen
Daniel Desjardins
Erica Crutchley
Jiraros Kewjaila
Kimball Gallagher
Panporn Puangchaipruek
Maitree and Peerapong Lekrungruangkit
Viswa Subbaraman
Neil Martin Rusell
Tasanee Sirikantraporn
Alan Ivory
Carol Kennedy
Vanasin Nalin

Naga (1,000)
(Anonymous)
Dr. Arnond Sakworanich
Chee Wong
Cipriano De Guzman Jr.
Divina Anatan
Kant Lormsomboon
Korn Lormsomboon
Ratana Roipornkasemsuk
Siriwat Chantaro
Thalassa Tapiia-Ruano Ferrand
Thidaporn Sermchai
Asaka Makino

Major Corporate Sponsors of the DasJati Project over the last five years

The following have generously donated funds or barter in order to aid the DasJati Project

The Department of Cultural Promotion
Ministry of Culture
Bangkok Metropolitan Administration
Thai Bev
B. Grimm
Rangsit University
Crown Property Bureau
Banyan Tree Hotel
Siam Kempinski Hotel
Thai Airways International
Asvanant Dental Clinic
Siam Commercial Bank
Bangkok Bank
Siam Cement Group
Pasaya
Arnoma Hotel
Pasaya
Etihad
Tourist Authority of Thailand
Bangkok Post
The Nation
River Engineering
Mahanakorn 3
PM Group
Thai Yarnyon
SparSha
Rockworth Office Systems
MTI
AIS
Centara Hotel
The Regents School

Members of the "Thanong 400"
a fund created by K Thanong where donors give 10,000 baht in exchange for a seat at all future performances of *DasJati* by Opera Siam for life

1. Tanong Platinumthailand
2. Chaiyoporn Chinaprayoon
3. Sasichome Noi Xoomsai
4. Big C Sukhsawat
5. Michael Proudfoot
6. Kanya Bunsupaporn
7. H.E. Dr. Peter Prügel
8. Somkiat Towanamchai
9. Anupong Khanthiphol
10 Dean Shibuya
11 Mink Sucharitkul
12. Thaithow Sucharitkul
13. Joey Shoji
14. Premika Sucharitkul
15-24. An Anonymous Donor
25. Supawan Napachotsiri
26. Thida Adireksarn
27. Andrew Biggs
28. Porama Chansue
29. Chalantorn Kaewtang
30. Soonthorn Asavanant
31. Yaowadee Yipintsoi
32. Klaomard Yipintsoi
33. Sompong Sucharitkul
34. Markus Thierstein
35. Maura Moynihan
36. Alan Ivory

www.ingramcontent.com/pod-product-compliance
Lightning Source LLC
Chambersburg PA
CBHW042017150426
43197CB00002B/57